The Whales

of
Tonga

Swimming
with
Pacific Nomads

by TIM ROCK
2021 Edition

Whales dance beneath the sea

Tim with whales in Ha'apai © Christian Jansen

ABOUT THIS BOOK

Say a warm "Malo e lelei (hello)" to one of the most welcoming countries in the South Pacific. The last Kingdom in the Pacific. And one of the last places on Earth a person can meet, face-to-face, one of the ocean's largest mammals... the humpback whale. Tonga. Sailors come to sail and party. Others drop out and drink kava. Locals live to praise the Lord with hauntingly beautiful choirs. Some come to stay in tidy lodges and wander deserted beaches. And whale lovers make the annual pilgrimage to see magnificent humpbacks.

While this book will feature the charming cultural and diverse geographic aspects of Tonga, the focus will mainly be on what to expect and do while interacting with the whales that come to Tonga for annual visits.

We'll discuss the behavior of these mammals that are as active at the surface as they are graceful underwater. And we'll look at what one can do to see the whales safely as well as look out for the whales' safety. It all goes hand-in-hand. And I'll relate a few tales about some of my favorite whale people and past humpback encounters.

Tonga is a place to enjoy whales, people and Nature and I guess that's why I think so highly of it.   - *Tim Rock*

A large juvenile humpback
frolics near the surface

A humpback breaches near a secluded Kapa area bay in Vava'u

A Guide to Enjoying

The WHALES of TONGA

Mother & baby and
snorkeler Yoko Higashide

About the Author:

Author Tim Rock

Tim Rock is an internationally published photojournalist who specializes in the ocean realm. Based on Guam in the Western Pacific Ocean, Rock has traveled Micronesia, the South Pacific, the Indo-Pacific and worldwide for four decades. He has visited Tonga many times to photograph the humpbacks and other marine life. He has published three other books about Tonga that can be found on Apple e-books and Amazon. He is a recipient of the University of Nebraska-Omaha Dept. of Communications Lifetime Achievement Award. He is the author of numerous Lonely Planet Diving & Snorkeling guides and has been featured in National Geographic Publications, Smithsonian and other major magazines. Tim offers a special thank you to **Yoko Higashide** for being such a great model and companion. Websites: **http://www. doubleblueimages.com** and **www.oceandreamspacific.com**

Humpback tail at sunset

The Whales of Tonga - Overview

Tonga is still new to tourism and is a bit of a diamond in the rough, which is part of its charm. We will focus on whale swimming and snorkeling. But Tonga has great hikes, healthy reefs and virtually untouched beaches as well as a special culture. People are friendly and quick to greet you with a "Malo e Lelei" (Good Day). Handicrafts are very nice and fresh fruits and some veggies come to market daily. It's a laid back and fascinating archipelago to visit.

Tonga's claim to fame for those wanting to be in the water with a whale is that it is one of the few places on the planet where it is legal to snorkel with these gentle giants. Various laws in other whale grounds around the world like Hawaii and Okinawa allow for whale watching, a fascinating experience in itself. But that way you only get to see half of what's going on. In Tonga, you can watch above and below. It's an exciting and often humbling and even life-changing experience.

While it may seem obvious, it is important to know that the whales are not in Tongan waters all year. June through October is when they are in Tonga with August and September

Utakalongalu Market in Vava'u

Tongatapu's stone trilithon...
the gateway Ha'amoga 'A Maui

considered to be the best months for whale swimming and action. Global warming is thought to have affected the feeding grounds to some extent in Antarctica, causing a decrease in food. In turn, reports are that the whales may be arriving later than June-July in the last couple years. So as we publish this book, we urge anyone planning to do anything whale related to check with your operator prior to buying tickets and arranging hotels. This may be just a seasonal glitch or it may mark a major change in the migration pattern.

Whale tourism is a huge international business nowadays with as many as ten million people annually participating in some sort of whale watching. But some countries still hunt whales and military sonar, pollution and global warming all threaten these large cetaceans. The International Fund for Animal Welfare (IFAW) is one of the most active organizations in the South Pacific region. It promotes conservation and awareness program for these whales and other marine mammals. To learn more, contact: **www.ifaw.org**.

The lifestyle here and the casual pace is part of the attraction. Tonga is a country that remains as close to the 'true' Polynesia as you're likely to find anywhere in the South Pacific. Tongans still live in village communities following traditional customs, especially on the outer islands. The distinctive traditional dress 'ta'ovala' – woven waist mats – are commonly worn. Meat and vegetables are still cooked in an underground oven called the 'Umu'. The ceremonial tradition of kava drinking is very much a

Soaking fibers to make the famous tapa cloth

Tongatapu has the ancient Langi (terraced tombs) of the Tongan kings

part of the daily lifestyle.

Tonga has remained true to its ancestral roots, partly because it is the only Pacific Island nation never colonized by a foreign power and it has also never lost its indigenous governance. After 1000 years of rule, today's monarchy and its structure still remain the most powerful and influential entity in Tonga.

Tongatapu's stone trilithon, gateway Ha'amoga 'A Maui (P. 8), dating back many centuries, stands as a powerful reminder of the legacy of this ancient and proud royal culture.

Recently, Tonga has been strongly influenced by Christianity. It may boast a record number of churches per capita. Melodic Sunday singing is ubiquitous.

Tonga Practicalities

History

Tonga has a rich history. The Tongan archipelago is thought to have been first inhabited somewhere between 3000 BC, and 1100 BC. Tongan warriors have been called "Vikings of the Pacific", attacking neighboring isles and extending the Tongan Empire to parts of Fiji, the Samoas, Tokelau and Niue.

Seemingly at random, first the Dutch and then the British turned up in Tonga round the 17th century. In the late 18th century Captain James Cook called Tonga the "Friendly Islands", a moniker that the islands retain to this day. No 19th Century power managed to set up a colonial administration here though many claimed the place. So it became a haven for the likes of pirates, deserters, whalers and blackbird slave traders, who infamously plundered some of Tonga's outer isles.

In the 1820s, missionaries changed another Pacific culture. Today, it is against the law to work on Sunday here. Western Religion and modesty reign.

Tonga's most renowned heroine may be Queen Salote. She was less interested in squabbles between churches and more in education and medicine for her people.

She was a popular queen who won friends for Tonga throughout the world and was mourned widely when she died in 1965. Her son, Taufa'ahau Tupou IV, ruled for 41 years. He died, age 88, on September 10, 2006. His son, Crown Prince Tupouto'a, was sworn in as King George Tupou V the following day. Westernized Tongans nowadays question the role of the monarchy, but Princess Pilolevu Tuita, daughter of Tupou IV, has been good for the whales.

Tongan ceremonial dance

At a Patron of Whales ceremony, she proclaimed Tonga a whale sanctuary and affirmed her father's decision to stop whale hunting over 45 years ago.

Today's Tongan monarchy remains an influential and powerful entity in the modern Kingdom, although one of the more contemporary Kings, George Tupou V, has introduced concessions to accommodate a more democratic state. As of the writing of this book, Tupou VI, son of Tāufaʻāhau Tupou IV, is the incumbent Tongan King. He served as Tonga's High Commissioner to Australia, and resided in Canberra until the death of King George Tupou V.

Historically, one of the most loved and admired members of the Tongan Royal Family was Queen Salote. Her choice to show respect by sitting in an uncovered carriage in pouring rain at the 1953 Coronation of Queen Elizabeth made her famous around the world.

The Royal Palace of the Kingdom of Tonga is located in the northwest of the capital, Nukuʻalofa, close to the ocean. The wooden Palace, which was built in 1867, is the official residence of the King of Tonga. Not open to the public, it is easily visible from the waterfront.

Leaving Sunday services (courtesy Tonga Tourism Authority)

Culture

Tongan society is guided by four core values, all of which combine to ensure a genuine welcome to visitors to the Kingdom. The four core values are Fefaka'apa'apa'aki (mutual respect), Feveitokai'aki (sharing, cooperating and fulfilment of mutual obligations), Lototoo (humility and generosity) and Tauhi vaha'a (loyalty and commitment).

Family is the central unit of Tongan life. Older people command the most respect and each family member knows his or her role. A typical family unit may consist of adopted children, cousins and other distant relatives, alongside siblings and grandparents.

The two biggest occasions for Tongan families are weddings and funerals where traditional tapa cloths and woven mats are gifted. Today, many Tongans still live in villages, and traditional village life has not changed greatly from earlier days. Many traditional practices are still an integral part of village life, making Tonga one of the most authentic traveller destinations in the South Pacific.

What to Know About Sunday

Visiting a church on Sunday is a treasured memory for many travellers to the Kingdom of Tonga. Sundays are devoted to church, family and rest, and, by law, work is not permitted. Beautifully clear harmonies, the ringing of church bells, and the rhythmic beat of the Lali (wooden drums), are all familiar sounds drifting on the tropical breezes. The islands resonate with hymns and harmonies every Sunday. Many visitors attend church and leave with special

Dancers perform wearing beautiful handmade tapa dresses and tekiteki headdresses

memories of the experience.

From the days of the early missionaries until modern times, Christianity has been a vital and influential aspect of Tongan life, second only to the respect for family. Modest dress is necessary for both Tongans and visitors.

All Closed

It is expected that visitors respect Sunday as a day of rest. Businesses and shops are closed by law allowing Tongan families to spend the day attending church for a relaxed day of worship and feasting. Whale swimming and scuba diving are kind of loosely associated with fishing, which is considered work. So plan your trips and days accordingly as there will be no whale trips done on a Sunday, even for visitors.

Sunday Flights

If you are planning to leave on a Monday, make sure you get down to Nuku'alofa by Saturday night. No local or international flights are scheduled on Sunday. Business contracts signed on a Sunday are legally void. It is a very respectful day and sports activities are not permitted, even in rugby-mad Tonga (visitors are permitted to enjoy all of the relaxing holiday activities provided by the resorts on Sunday and some businesses like restaurants open on

Necklaces made from cow and old whale bone in Nuka'alofa

Sunday night, but not a lot).

Handicrafts

Tongan arts and handicrafts, including bone carving, wood carving, basket making and fine weaving are made using techniques passed down through generations of Tongan craftspeople. They are found in resorts and craft shops and in the various market stalls. They make beautiful keepsakes to remind travellers of time spent here.

One of the most famous local crafts is the making of tapa, a decorative bark cloth painted with traditional symbols and designs. Tapa is usually offered as a gift of respect at weddings, births and funerals.

Like tapa making, mat weaving is an everyday part of Tongan life. Women gather in small groups to weave, sing or talk together. Mats are the most treasured possessions in Tongan households and are also traditionally presented at births, weddings, funerals

Some beautiful woven and tapa items

and other special occasions.

Tongans also wear mats known as the 'ta'ovala' around the waist as a respectful form of dress in the Kingdom. This custom originated in ancient times when men returning after long voyages at sea, would cut the mast sails of their canoes and cover their naked bodies prior to appearing before their chief.

Finely woven mats – 'ta'ovala' – are particularly treasured. They are handed down from generation to generation, some dating back hundreds of years.

Another vibrant and colorful experience for many visitors to Tonga is the graceful and dignified dancing of the Kingdom. Dancers step their feet and move their arms gracefully (women) and vigorously (men), complemented by

traditional wear, beautiful bracelets, neck garlands and the tekiteki (a feather headpiece), creating another memorable expression of local culture and tradition.

Food

Traditional Tongan favorites to try include 'ota 'ika (raw fish marinated in lemon and coconut cream) which is incredibly delicious. There's also lu pulu (corned beef and coconut milk wrapped in taro leaves). Food and feasting are an integral part of Tongan society. Some of the hotels have a "Tongan night' where all the favorite local foods are offered. There are also a few independent cultural performances that come with a great variety of dancing, local music

Musicians and singers gather around the kava bowl

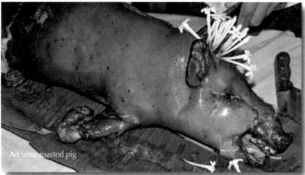

An umu roasted pig

part of life in the Kingdom of Tonga. The homegrown product is renowned across the Pacific, with the finest kava in Tonga reputedly being produced from the fertile soils of the volcanic islands of Tofua in the Ha'apai group and Tafahi in Niuatoputapu.

and a sampling of the food. Try the local food if you can... highly recommended.

Try the Kava too

You can't go anywhere in Tonga without seeing people partaking around the old kava bowl. Ceremonial drinking of kava is an ancient custom undertaken across all of Polynesia and is an integral

Tongan villages have at least one kava club (kava kulupu) and they're popular venues after dark for local men. Most every night, you will see people on porches sitting around the kava bowl as you stroll the neighborhoods. Tongans will gather at street corners or in a front yard and sip the kava, play musical instruments like ukeleles or guitars and sing songs with beautiful harmonies.

Kava is also drunk before and after church on a Sunday, during the conferment of nobility and at village meetings.

It is kind of a muddy-looking liquid made from the leaves of the pepper plant, but drinking it at least once is an essential experience for visitors to Tonga. It is drunk from a coconut shell and it can quickly relax the body

A table full of tongan delicacies

and makes your tongue and lips go numb. But you get a nice, relaxed feeling, which may be why the whole Tongan vibe is so laid back.

Tongans also do some great dishes with fish. Add in some coconut milk, taro leaves and various starches such as yams, taro, sweet potatoes and tapioca and you have a hearty Tongan repast. And try the feke, which is a grilled octopus or squid also prepared in a coconut sauce.

Beachfront drive in Tongatapu

Getting There

Tongatapu is the Kingdom's largest and most populous island. It is the capital and the main center of government and business. You will most likely arrive in Tonga here at Fua'amotu International Airport, Tonga's main airport and international gateway. The airport is about 13 miles (21km) from the main town of Nuku'alofa. This is where the most hotels and restaurants are located, although there are resorts in other parts of Tongatapu and on some offshore islets. You can get a taxi or have your hotel arrange a pickup for you. The drive into town takes you past some villages and fields, then along the sea until you get into the city. As of this writing, direct services to Tongatapu are operated by Air New Zealand, Fiji Airways, Virgin Australia and Talofa Airways.

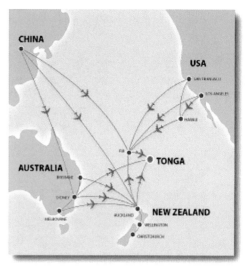

There are separate International and Domestic terminals at the airport. Regular domestic services are operated by Real Tonga Airlines to Vava'u, Ha'apai & 'Eua. And there are less frequent services to northern Niuatoputapu and Niuafo'ou.

Fiji is the main gateway to Tonga. It is only 90 minutes away by air. If you are coming from the USA, there are flights to Fiji from San Francisco, Los Angeles or Hawaii. Or you can transit via New Zealand. The flight from Auckland to Tonga takes under three hours. You can also fly directly to Tonga from Sydney, Australia. From Asia, fly from South Korea or Hong Kong to Sydney, Auckland or Fiji then on to Tonga. Check updated airline schedules and COVID entry requirements before you travel. There is a TOP $25 departure tax payable in cash. You will also need to complete a Passenger Departure Card before passing through security.

Enjoying the countryside by bike on the way to the store

The "country" aspect of Tonga can be seen as kids move stock by horseback

Domestic Air Travel

Real Tonga is Tonga's national domestic carrier and it has a bit of a sour reputation for cancellations... so make sure you have a bit of flexibility in your flight schedule in Tonga as in-country flights do change. Travel insurance is recommended.
Website: https://realtonga.to

Getting Around

A Visitor's Driving License is a must in Tonga. This allows travellers with overseas licenses to drive in the country legally, but a license is not hard to obtain. They are available to purchase from the Ministry of Infrastructure building in Nuku'alofa or the Police Station in Neiafu. Alternatively, some car rental companies and hotels with rental cars in Tongatapu have a permit to issue a driving license for a fee.

You don't need to take any test but you must be 18-years-old or over and present your valid license from your home country.

Accommodation

From village homestays and simple guesthouses to private eco-resorts and lodges, the Kingdom of Tonga offers accommodation options for travelers of all budgets and preferences. The accommodation is often located on remote, pristine islands or on sweeping

Kids coming home on Sunday from church in Neiafu.

world-class beaches. Most are locally owned, guaranteeing a warm Tongan welcome. Active adventure and passive relaxation is on tap, always delivered with traditional Tongan hospitality and warmth. Tonga's whale season is short and hotels, restaurants and whale operations tend to close down or change hands from one year to the next, so we include no listings in this book. It is best to check and see which accommodations are operating well before the season starts, however. They fill up quickly, especially the ones with good reputations and reasonable costs.

Climate and Dress

Tonga looks tropical but leans a bit toward temperate. Days can be warm to downright hot, especially out in a boat. But, evenings may require a light jacket or sweater. The best months to travel are July through November. It can get hot in the summer (and there's no whales), but seldom reaches above 95°F (35°C). Trade winds from the east-southeast bring cooling breezes in the late afternoon and early evening. Tropical rains fall from December through February. However, there are no significant differences in temperatures.

Practical and modest dress is necessary for both Tongans and visitors. Allowances are made for tourists at beaches and beach resorts. But you will see most Tongans are conservatively covered even when at the beach. On a

Ocean-loving pigs at sunset on Tongatapu

boat while whale watching and swimming, the water reflects the sun. Wear proper sunscreen, hats, longsleeve shirts and other sun protection. We'll discuss water temps in the photo section.

Electricity

The power in Tonga is 240 volts, using the same angled 2 & 3 pronged plug common to New Zealand and Australia. There is a hardware store in Nuku'alofa but few other adapter options so it is best to bring a few with you.

Visa

Tourist visas are good for 30 days and given to most visitors without hassle.

Language

Tongan is the official language of the country but English is also widely spoken.

Currency

The Tongan Pa'anga is the local currency. New Zealand and Australian dollars can also be used. There are banks and ATMs in major whale watching towns and established hotels and restaurants take major credit cards. B&Bs and homestays may require cash.

For more information visit Tonga's Visitors Bureau Website:
http://www.tongaholiday.com

A healthy, growing "baby" humpback plays at the surface

Whale Swimming - The Rules

The Kingdom of Tonga is made up of 171 islands, sprawling across the South Pacific Ocean. And around most of these islands, in season, you'll find whales. Whale swimming in Tonga occurs when whales have migrated to mate and calve.

To protect these natural behaviors, a set of rules has been created. The only way you are legally able to swim with whales in Tonga is to do a tour with a licensed operator who abides by a set of regulations. This keeps both customers and the whales happy and safe.

Everyone on a licensed whale

swimming tour is briefed regarding what they can and can't do during the whale swim. These rules are in place not only to keep the whales safe but to also keep humans safe. I do not know of any recorded whale attacks around Tonga, but I do know of an incident on my home island of Guam. A friend of mine, who was videotaping whales, went too close to a humpback calf and the mother took a swipe at him with her pectoral fin to shoo him out of the way. This resulted in some nasty cuts on his torso from the barnacles on the fin.

We also had an incident where a

Snorkeling along with mother and calf

sperm whale hit a diver who was too close to a newborn calf. As some whales weigh as much as 40 tons, they are not creatures with whom you want to have even accidental contact.

So these rules have been devised to protect the whales and the swimmers/snorkelers.

1) Swimmers are dropped off no closer than 33ft (10m) away from whales and 165 ft (50m) from whales with calves

2) Swimmers can approach whales no closer than 15 feet (5m)

3) In he water, swimmers are to stay with the guide at all times

4) Swimmers are to listen to the guide's instructions

5) Only four swimmers (and the guide... five total) can be in with the whale at one time

6) Don't jump from the boat into the water. Slide in quietly.

Whale tours operators will not approach a whale if it is displaying any unsafe behavior, such as breaching. But this is the time to get your surface action shots of these huge creatures leaping from the sea.

The skipper will determine whether it is appropriate to swim with the whale or not. If so, swimmers will be required to put on masks and fins quickly and get in the water, four swimmers at one time only. There may be a lot of getting in and out of the water, depending on how fast the whale is moving or if it proves to not be a good whale to swim with and another whale needs to be found.

A curious calf watches as a snorkeler approaches

If the whale does prove to be good to swim with, swimmers will be required to follow the guide during the experience. The guide will make sure swimmers are an appropriate distance away from the whale (16ft/5m or more). Follow the advice of your whale swimming guides and skippers. Some guides seem to know how and where the whales swim even though you are snorkeling like crazy but just seeing blue water. Keep and eye on the guide's fins and follow. If you don't, you'll get a lot of exercise but probably won't see many humpbacks. The seas in Tonga can get high and rough. Wear a wetsuit or something that aids in your floatation and perhaps a bright hood so you can be spotted easily if you get

separated from the group.

While many whale operators in Tonga run tours with the whales' well-being in mind, not all toe the line. Recent studies in the Vava'u group have shown that some operators do not follow the regulations. The Tongan government capped the number of whale licenses given out annually to not exceed 7 for Tongatapu, 20 for Vava'u, 10 for Ha'apai and 4 for 'Eua. Some operators feel added pressure to provide a good whale swim for customers, especially those customers just doing one day tours as as many as eight people (two groups) may be on their boats. Also, some flout restrictions, such as the time spent with the whales, which has shown to have a negative impact on whale mothers and their calves. By carefully selecting an ethical whale operator, you can choose a more eco-friendly tour that operates with the whales' well-being in mind.

The government also has a Whale Enforcement Team inspecting boats each morning to record that the appropriate certified skippers and staff are working on the boats.

Seeing humpbacks often involves swimming in the open water where swells are present. Sometimes these can be quite big and rough on a windy, Tongan day. Needless to say, you then need to be a strong swimmer to enjoy this experience. If you are not comfortable in big seas, don't go in.

Snorkelling gear is normally available if you don't have your own, including mask, snorkel, fins and a wetsuit.

Allow one or two days to be free both before and after the date of a pre-booked whale swim in case your tour is rescheduled due to weather conditions. This does happen. If serious about whale swimming, charter a boat for the entire week and split the costs with your group of friends. The more time on the sea, the more chance there is of having a fantastic whale encounter during your Tonga visit.

Mother and calf snuggle as the escort watches. Keeping a proper distance while whale swimming allows the whales to be themselves.

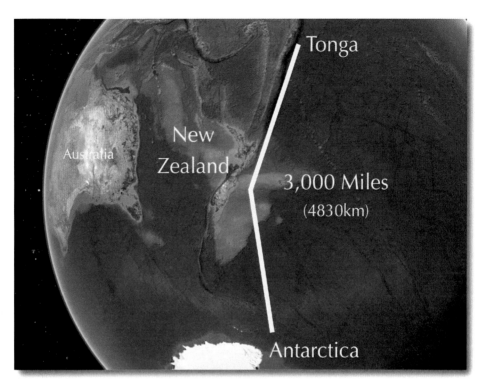

Tonga

New Zealand

Australia

3,000 Miles
(4830km)

Antarctica

Where Do the Whales Come From?

The Great Migration

Whale migrations take place in all seas and rival or surpass overland and better-known mass migrations, such as the great wildebeest marches across Africa's Serengeti.

Tonga's whales travel huge distances twice a year. Antarctica is their feeding ground and Tonga is their mating and calving ground. The distance from one place to the next is about 3000 miles (roughly 4830km). When leaving Tonga they follow the Tonga Trench, which is the second deepest in the world. They pass New Zealand and eventually wind up in a feeding area in northern Antarctica. Not much is known about this route or why they have chosen it. But now scientists believe they also follow a series of sea mounts, resting and possibly feeding along the way.

The whales must eat enough during their Antarctic stay to 'fast' for six to eight months while they migrate to the warmer waters to give birth, mate, then migrate back down to the feeding grounds in the Antarctic again.

Climate change has some scientists worried about what the future holds for the whales. As global ocean temperatures increase, this may alter the

Mother and calf make the
long journey to Antarctica

A large blow from a rising humpback

humpbacks' migration between Antarctica and Oceania. This is due to changes in their food sources, mainly krill, which are being impacted. Global warming and overfishing have both already been blamed for a dramatic fall in krill numbers. The ice that is home to the algae and plankton that krill feed on is melting.

According to The Guardian, krill are a key part of the delicate Antarctic food chain. They feed on marine algae and are a key source of food for whales, penguins and seals. They are also important in removing the greenhouse gas carbon dioxide from the atmosphere by eating carbon-rich food near the surface and excreting it when they sink to lower, colder water.

Humpback whales need to feed intensively throughout the summer and autumn, as they generally are thought to fast during migration and on the breeding grounds and rely on fat reserves for energy during those months. However, there is evidence that at least some individuals from some populations forgo migration altogether in some years and remain on feeding grounds throughout the winter months.

A Milky Way sky with Vava'u whales seemingly enjoying the stars.... scientific studies suggest humpbacks sleep at night for short periods at or near the surface. They also have dreams.

Humpback Facts

Scientific name: *Megaptera novaeangliae*, meaning "Great wings of New England"
Type of whale: Baleen whale
Birth weight and size: About 1.5 tons and 10 to 16ft (3-4.5m) long
Size after first year: Doubled
Sexual maturity weight and size:
Females: About 45 tons and 45ft (1.5m) long
Males: About 42 tons and 42ft (12.5m) long
Sexual maturity age: 5 to 9 years
Life span: Estimated to be 40 to 50+ years
Gestation: 10 to 12 months
Calving interval: 1 to 3 years
Life cycle: Breeds, calves and nurses in Tonga the winter/spring (June thru October), then migrates to Antarctica to feed in the summer.
Diet: Krill, plankton and small fish (have been seen possibly feeding in Tonga)
- The whale pectoral fin is the longest in the animal kingdom. It has the same amount of bones as the human hand. So they are closer to us than you think!

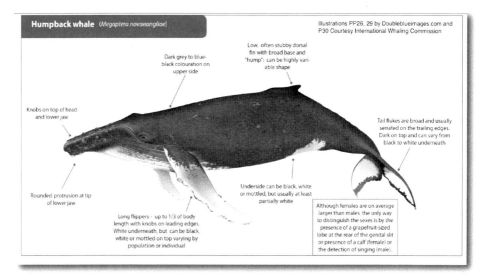

Humpback whale *(Megaptera novaeangliae)*

Illustrations PP26, 29 by Doubleblueimages.com and P30 Courtesy International Whaling Commission

Dark grey to blue-black colouration on upper side

Low, often stubby dorsal fin with broad base and "hump"; can be highly variable shape

Knobs on top of head and lower jaw

Tail flukes are broad and usually serrated on the trailing edges. Dark on top and can vary from black to white underneath

Rounded protrusion at tip of lower jaw

Underside can be black, white or mottled, but usually at least partially white

Long flippers - up to 1/3 of body length with knobs on leading edges. White underneath, but can be black, white or mottled on top varying by population or individual

Although females are on average larger than males, the only way to distinguish the sexes is by the presence of a grapefruit-sized lobe at the rear of the genital slit or presence of a calf (female) or the detection of singing (male).

Shifts in ocean productivity, a result of climate change and possibly overfishing the krill, have almost certainly played a role in some of the recently observed changes or anomalies in migration patterns and feeding grounds. So folk in Tonga and other places with whale tourism are watching closely to see if this affects arrivals and departures.

Also, in southeast Australia, whales have been seen forming what are called super groups (more than 20 whales). In one instance in September 2020, more than 100 whales were in a super group. This huge group has been seen feeding using the bubble net strategy that was previously only observed in use by them in Antarctica. It's possible that, as whale numbers return, we are seeing them perform group behaviors from the time before they were hunted so extensively. Or it could be that a boom in whale babies in this tribe created a need for more feeding.

Until very recently, humpback whales were thought to be 'feast and famine' feeders who will fast during migration. But new observations challenge that. Very little is actually known about how whales interact during the actual migration run in the open sea.

Having arrived in Tonga after their amazing journey, the humpbacks head for their breeding grounds to give birth and mate. Some whales show up as early as June. Normally, the season runs from July to October.

A pregnant female will feed intensively for several months in order to gain sufficient strength and body mass for successful birth and lactation. In Antarctica, you will probably see pregnant females arriving earlier than males, non-pregnant females and juveniles. Then she returns to the Tongan breeding ground to give birth after gestation of approximately 11.5 months.

Humpbacks also need strength just for

Newborn calves are lighter in color

the trip. The average migration speed of a whale is a continuous 3-to-7-miles-per-hour (5-11kph) with very few stops. That's quite an impressive daily clip to maintain.

Males in Tonga will engage in aggressive competition to gain access to females. Swimmers in the water will also hear the males singing. They produce long complex songs, with all males in the population singing roughly the same song, but slowly changing it over the course of the season. Depending on the hull structure of your boat, you may hear these songs reverberating through the ship. During breeding season the males are known for singing the longest and most complex songs in the animal kingdom.

Humpback whales are wide ranging and can be found virtually worldwide, but with apparent geographical segregation between at least ten populations. The whales in Tonga have been dubbed the Tonga Tribe. Now Tonga's whales may number as many as 1000. It is likely that there were 10,000 in that tribe alone before whaling decimated them. 100,000 humpbacks were killed by whalers throughout the modern whaling era and, although some stocks seem to be recovering, today's population is still a fraction of its original size. The Tonga Tribe was finally fully protected in 1978. There were roughly only 250 left by then.

The Tonga Tribe has rebounded well over the years although not as robust as some of the neighboringSouth Pacific tribes. This double annual migration is what makes humpback whales worldwide so special.

Near sunset, a humpback calf breaches

Whale Behavior

Humpback whales are one of the most-watched and well-studied species of whale. They are in every ocean and many nearshore areas associated with coastal and marine tourism. They are the focus of whale watching operations in many cities and countries around the world. The species is known for its spectacular "surface active behavior", which can include breaching (leaping clear of the water) and flipper and tail slapping and its occasional curiosity around boats and snorkelers. The whales can also be heard singing complex 'song' while you are in the water or even aboard your

A breaching humpback whale

Humpback pectoral fin bones are similar to human hands

boat. It is magnified by boat's hull. Song seems to form during migration and is heard in the breeding grounds. Humpbacks have a range that covers eight octaves, from a bass so low that humans can't hear it to a magnificent soprano. Their highly structured songs include multiple themes that are constantly repeated and even rhyme. The songs last up to 30 minutes and they also improvise, like in jazz music.

The Tongan group is no exception. They are known for spectacular breaching, flipper-slapping and tail lobbing. A humpback is easily identified at close range by its knobby head and long flippers, so is not even close to a dolphin or other marine mammal. The black and white coloration on the underside of the flukes (tail) allows scientists to distinguish and name individuals all around the world. Like a human fingerprint, no two humpback whale tails are exactly alike.

A humpback whale's blow or the splash of a breach can be seen from a long distance and a good boat captain with a good boat will try to hurry to get you to the show.

Here are some terms used to describe the activity whales display on the surface:

Blow: This is a cloud or column of moist air forcefully expelled through the blowhole when the whale surfaces to breathe. When a whale dives, air is compressed in its lungs. Upon reaching

Whales take a peek above the surface by spyhopping

large blows and a small one may be a whale couple with calf, etc.

Breaching: This is a calculated leap out of the water, exposing the majority of its body. The more spectacular jumps may see the whale completely out of the ocean. The main reason for breaching (and tail/pectoral slapping) is communication. But it may also serve to dislodge remoras. Mothers will teach calves to breach and once a calf catches on, it may do as many 50 jumps of its newly found trick.

Flukes: These are the flat horizontal lobes that form the tail of all whale and dolphin species.

the surface, the air is exhaled through the whale's blowholes. The exhaled air expands, causing the temperature to decrease, thereby condensing into water vapor. The blow is quite visible and can reach heights of 20 feet (6m).

For some species of whale, like humpbacks, this can be seen from far away. It is also sometimes referred to as a **spout**. Your operator will be able to tell if a small blow and large blow take place, indicating mother and calf. Two

Fluking/Sounding: Photographers love to get a nice shot of this activity. When a whale or dolphin begins a deep dive, it lifts its tail into the air to help it thrust its body into a more steeply angled descent to deeper waters. The last thing exposed is the tail.

Lobtailing: You will see the whales forcefully slapping the flukes against the surface of the water.

Pec-slapping: This is raising a flipper out of the water and slapping it noisily against the water's surface.

Pectoral fins: Although often referred to as fins – these are actually modified limbs with bone structures much like

Tail slapping and lobtailing are other forms of whale communication

Double fluking with two whales sounding

A playful whale with both fins out of the sea

human's arms and hands. They are used for stability and steering, and are more appropriately called flippers.

Peduncle-slapping/peduncle throw:

This is also known as tail-breaching, throwing the rear portion of the body out of the water and slapping it sideways onto the surface, or on top of another whale. It can be used in heat run fights.

Spyhop: a behavior where a whale or dolphin raises its head vertically above the water, then slips back below the surface. Whales can see well above the water and sometimes come up to see what's going on.

Whale: This term is used to refer to any large cetacean, but technically scientists distinguish between toothed cetaceans (*odontocetes*) and those (like humpbacks) with baleen plates instead of teeth (mysticetes).

There are many other behaviors you may see as well. Not far from Vava'u's harbor, we watched as a late afternoon rain poured down. A calf held its head above the surface to feel the gentle, tropical drops, then opened it's mouth to taste fresh water for what was probably the first time in its life. The surprises never end.

No monopod on board... no problem! Clark Miller uses Douglas Hoffman as a duopod while shooting above water action.

Whale Photography - Above

Humpback whales present a unique challenge to photographers due to the fact as they can be as entertaining above water as they are below. When you go diving, chances are that almost 100% of your subjects will be underwater. And if you go on an animal safari, your subjects almost 100% of the time will be flying through the air or grazing and hunting on land. Not so with whales. One moment, they can be playing on the surface or breaching. The next moment, they may decide to swim right under the boat. And you have to: a) Be VERY ready for both. b) React. If there is breaching happening, you need to have your camera with the telephoto lens and rapid fire capability up to your eye and ready to rock or have your video rolling. A huge whale breaching lasts but split seconds. It is up in the air and back into the sea before you can blink. You have to have line of sight, the lens in sharp focus and the photo at least somewhat framed. It isn't easy.

In nice weather on a small boat with a small amount of folks, this is a challenge but not a huge one. On a small boat with 8-10 people all jockeying for position, it is even more of a mess. In rough weather, possibly with wind and rain, it is even harder and most "land"

Getting a nice tail shot is one above-water image that can be captured from a boat.

cameras are not well-sealed for exposure to the elements. The boat is rocking up and down, rain droplets are getting on the front of your lens or lens filter, the whales are appearing and then disappearing. You get a lot of shots of the sky and out-of-focus ocean.

And, oddly, whales seem to like to play on rough days. So that super breach you always wanted to capture may take place in the worst of the weather.

If you have a tough camera like an Olympus Tough or other such rugged camera, then you are somewhat ahead of the game. Same with a GoPro or similar action cam. You don't have to worry as much about water damage or banging the lens or body as the waves toss you about. But to really get great shots of whales, a higher end mirrorless or DSLR camera (a camera without a fixed lens), is still pretty much a requirement. And you have to be steady on top of all that. Monopods and tripods (if you have the room) can help. Sometimes it is all but impossible.

Then, good weather or bad, you may hear the call from the captain, "Get Ready!!". And in that instant, you know he has deemed it possible to get in the water with the whales. You don't have time to leisurely put away your camera and break out your underwater gear and garb. In reality, you should be wearing it. On hot days, this means you can be frying in your wetsuit while you are trying to shoot the whales above the surface. On wet days, it is usually a welcome move to be suited up on the windy or rainy deck.

When you hear his warning, you have

Whale swimming means you have to always be ready to jump in. Here Douglas Hoffman already has his mask, hood and wetsuit on as he shoots topside action with a VR lens.

to secure your expensive above water camera gear as quickly as possible, grab your underwater camera, which you have set up in advance, get into your fins, mask and snorkel and be ready to quietly slide, not jump, into the sea. It is organized insanity at its finest. Once in the water, you then have to find the whales, which may be coming your way or may have already passed.

Now, what to use above the surface for this jostle with Mother Nature? Your choice of lens is the most important decision you'll make when it comes to being able to fill the frame with your subject. You'll want to use a **zoom lens**, because you never know when the wildlife will decide to check out the boat you're in. Some options to think about: a focal length range of around 55-200mm, 70-300mm, 28-300mm all the way up to the 200-500mm lens. When using a full frame camera, you can manually set the camera to a shooting mode and that will give you a 1.5x crop factor which will effectively give you a little bit more zoom reach. Cropped sensor cameras automatically add the 1.5x crop factor onto the focal length of a lens. For example, using the 200-500mm will give you a zoom range of 300-750mm. You may end up doing a lot of your shooting at the telephoto end, but don't discount the wider end of the zoom which you can use to show the breadth of the ocean and the animals who live there (see pages 4 & page 41).

If you're using a VR **(Vibration Reduction image stabilization)** built-in lens on your camera, you'll want to turn ON the VR. If your lens also gives you the option of selecting from Active or Normal and you're taking pictures from a boat, set the VR setting to Active. This can help compensate for the movement of the boat.

If you want the camera to do the heavy lifting for you, so you don't want to have to think about settings, set the camera to **Sports Mode** if it has scene modes. If it doesn't have any scene modes, set the camera to **Auto or Program**.

If you're comfortable setting the exposure manually go ahead and do so; or use shutter priority in which you set the **shutter speed** and the camera selects the appropriate aperture. You'll want to use a relatively fast shutter speed to be able to freeze the action of whales breaching, slapping their tails or slapping pectoral fins on the water. The shutter speed should be 1/500 or faster. Using a smaller aperture will give you more depth of field in your images.

If you're setting your exposure manually, set the **ISO** high enough for the available light to allow you to use the shutter speed and aperture combination you want to freeze the action. This is imperative as whale shots above and below can easily be victims of blur from a too low shutter speed. If it is cloudy and the sun is often breaking through and then disappearing again,

Sunny and calm days are blessings for above water shooting

set the camera to **Auto ISO**. The camera will adjust the ISO based on the amount of light and readjust when the sun is obscured and the light level drops. For **white balance**, set the camera to **Auto** or, if it's sunny, to direct sunlight (this may just be a symbol of a bright sun). If its cloudy or overcast set it to **Cloudy** (symbol of a sun and a cloud).

Remember, a **small aperture** of f/6.3 to f/11 is preferred with humpbacks due to their size, and it allows for most of the whale to be in focus. If a whale comes close and you have a wide aperture of f/4 it will result in just a small area of the whale being in focus. This can be good to isolate a particular feature, but if you want a pec or tail shot use a smaller aperture like f/11 to ensure

the majority of your image will be sharp.

Breaching whales are always amazing to see, but it can be difficult to capture the leap. They can jump unexpectedly, without any notice and close to you, making it nearly impossible to capture. This is where your GoPro set at 4K may come in handy. If close enough, you may be able to grab a frame from the video of your action cam instead of fumbling with focus and focal length. But practice will make perfect. You will get better and faster with shooting stills the more your push yourself to master getting a properly framed, sharp image.

Sometimes they breach many times. If so, having a lens over 400mm narrows your field of view and makes it hard to

Whitecaps and whale tails... the seas can be challenging at times

find the whale. Having a shorter lens (70-200) widens your chances of capturing the action. You can crop a bit if needed afterwards.

If you can see a whale is moving in a particular direction, move your focus point and compose your image while the whale is underwater. This means you're ready to grab proper focus and fire the shutter at a moment's notice should it jump.

Whales are big animals, but not as big as the ocean they live in. **Wide lenses** (18-300) are perfect for environment images. These are important to get as they help you tell a story. They help show the whale's surroundings and help the viewer understand better.

A day on the ocean may mean sun and rain in the same day. And it may mean rough seas (meaning lots of saltwater splashes). A couple of **dry bags** and a few small, dry cloths, like wash cloths, are really valuable to keep land cameras dry and to secure them quickly should it rain or you have to jump in .

You can always get an environment type of photo with a wider lens or wide zoom setting

41

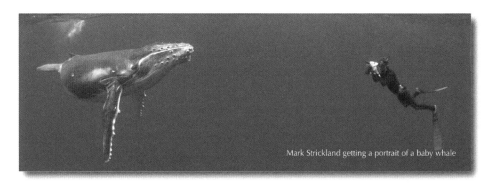

Mark Strickland getting a portrait of a baby whale

Whale Photography - Below

A guy named Howard Hall, who shoots many of the underwater IMAX movies seen worldwide, once wrote a book about how to improve your underwater photography. He and his wife Michele recently produced a wonderful movie simply called "Whales" that is truly beautiful and available to be seen online. In his book, his number one underwater photography tip is (who woulda thought?): **Get in the Water!!** It makes no difference how fancy your camera is and how strong your lights are and how expensive your wide angle lens is. If they are sitting in the hotel room, you're not shooting.

The same applies for photographing whales. Your trip is long and not cheap and with off days due to rough weather and no swimming on Sundays, whale time can also be limited. The next whale encounter may be the "Best Ever"!!

Go out looking for whales as often as you can and stay out as long as you can and get in the water as often as you can.

Ed Yoblonski has his camera preset and at the ready for word to slide in to swim with the humpbacks.

You never know when some whales will do something really special right in front of your lens. But you do have to be out there to be in the water to have and capture the super cool experience.

Now, most whale photography is done by snorkeling unless you are lucky enough to have whales pass by while

Some lighting help from above shines on this mother and calf.

you are making a dive on scuba. So practice, practice, practice snorkeling before you come to Tonga so your stamina is good and you can take advantage of every moment.

Dress

Dress for success as well. Wear at least a 2-3mil top or vest as Tonga's waters are around 73-79F (23-26C) during whale season. If you have a good encounter, you don't want to have to get out of the water just because you feel cold. Get something like a Lavacore vest that also offers wind protection and warmth when you are on the boat and dripping wet. A freediving weight belt made of rubber is also more

comfortable than a diver's weight belt. You don't really need to freedive down on whales. In fact, some captains/guides won't allow it. But having a little weight on helps you to simply exhale and sink below the surface just enough to get a new perspective when shooting. This is actually pretty important. Also, get in the water slowly and quietly. A big splash scares whales.

Time of the Season

If all goes well, the whales should arrive starting in June and July and the pregnant mothers will have a calf after arriving. You can expect the mothers to be very protective of their babies and not stay around humans much when

Playful calves make great photo subjects

approached by swimmers. But as the season goes on, that calf will gain at least 100 pounds (45kg) per day and become more curious, playful and adventurous. Mom will do her best to keep the calf in line, but she has to be aware of its antics 24-hours-a-day. After a couple to three months, mom is tired. She may actually just take a nap while the baby comes up to play with snorkelers. And she may be more used to swimmers by then and even a bit curious herself. Thus, the best months for whale swimming are normally August and September if you are trying to get images of mother and calf. Also, by late September into October, the mom and baby may have picked up an escort so you could have a whale "family" to photograph. The key is to get into the water and see what surprises each day holds, be it June or October. Once the whales start to move on the way to their southern feeding grounds, they are less cooperative. They are in the mode to cover many miles each day and interactions may turn more into fly-bys until the Tongan waters are silent and the whales are out to open sea heading to Antarctica again.

Cameras

Kind of like what we discussed in the "Above" section, cameras will generally come down to action cams and DSLR/Mirrorless. People can use GoPros or DJI Osmo Action as they are

Swimming and snapping away along with a mother and calf

waterproof down to 24-30 feet (8-9m) or so without a case. They can get a housing for an iPhone/SmartPhone or use something like an Olympus Tough waterproof camera. All of these items are small and easy to drop into the deep blue abyss. Get a lanyard and a float for them.

About the worst thing that can happen is that bubbles can get on the front of the lens. So check to make sure your still or video masterpiece isn't going to be screwed up by a couple of bubbles on the front lens. Check frequently. This also goes for the big domes for DSLR/Mirrorless cams. Some photographers also mount action cams to the big housings so they can shoot video and stills at the same time.

For more serious photographers, a good camera in a good housing is a must. Lights are not necessary

and may be frowned on by your guide. A small, compact housing, even a surf housing, for your camera is best and

Converting to Black & White can create dramatic whale images

Scott Harrison, at the ready, waits for the word to gently slide in. One of the crew will then hand him the camera.

make sure your camera body can shoot continuously. Also make sure your camera can write to the SD card quickly and ensure this. Get a fast, high quality SD card or two.

The ISO largely depends on lighting conditions, but ISO 400 is a safe number that should ensure no grain but still some speed. As cameras improve, many can easily go to 800 or 1600 ISO without adding grain/color noise to the image. Use the fastest continuous frame rate (ideally at least in the 4–14fps range) in continuous shooting mode to capture the action.

Lens?

I use both a 10-17mm and a 7-14mm on a mirrorless camera. An MFT lens is the same as a full frame lens with twice the focal length. So, roughly 20-34 and 14-28 in focal length. My friends with full frame cameras prefer a 16–35mm lens, which is similar. You can always zoom out if you get close to keep the water column between the whale and your camera to a minimum. But for shy whales, or even portrait situations, you can zoom. No matter what camera you use, action or pro style, try to get as close as the guide allows. This makes an immense difference in image quality. The ability to zoom to longer focal lengths is helpful but not to be regularly practiced. As in all underwater photography, get close to reduce the

Matching surface light and the deep blue below is a challenge of whale photography

focus point at any time and then recompose or just hold the button down for continuous AF.

Activate all AF points and let the camera focus on the part of the whale that is closest to the camera. Getting in the right position is important and a huge challenge. Keep the sun at your back as best you can. Even with no flash, sun on particles in the water creates backscatter and can ruin a great whale image.

Whales are faster than you think so have everything set up before you hit the water and then while kicking along try to be as steady as you can to ensure both sharp and well-composed whale images of your adventure.

amount of water between the lens and the subject.

There are domes for GoPros and wide angle attachments for camera housings for cameras like iPhones and the Tough. DSLR/Mirrorless cameras should have a wide dome (perhaps 8") for the best image quality and the ability to shoot split shots. Companies like G-Dome make a light, handy housing that adapts to a number of small cameras.

Settings

A shutter speed of 1/100 to 1/250 should stop motion for wide lenses and if light is in short supply you can extend this to 1/60s but really hold that camera steady. If the subject is moving this could be tough. Shoot at F6.3 or F8.

If your camera displays a histogram, refer to it. LCD screens can be misleading underwater. Set the drive to Continuous. Then you can take one shot or many. This is key... set up the camera ahead of time so you can activate the autofocus from the AF button (back button focus) allowing you to lock the

Editing

For still photos, be prepared to spend a bit of time in Photoshop or your favorite digital darkroom. Shoot in RAW if possible to capture more detail and greater dynamic range from your camera sensor. RAW also allows more flexibility for editing. Whale images are largely blue, black and white. The sunlight strength on the surface dictates the broad range of extremes of color and light patterns. Overcast days are actually good days for near surface photography. Many photographers prefer to turn their images into black and white photos. The final images can be very dramatic presented in B&W.

A male grabs a quick breath
and then joins a female

A moment of awe by both snorkeler and calf

Video

Most DSLRs also have excellent video features nowadays. So stills and videos can be made both above and underwater. One suggestion is to decide which you want to concentrate on and stick with it. If you try to do both sometimes you can miss the best part while you're trying to decide which to do. The best thing you can do, especially with video, is start the recording to get the best footage.

But if a moment presents itself that may be better on stills than video (or vice-versa), it is nice to know you have the option to switch. Just make sure your fiddling around doesn't cost you both the still and the video sequence and leave you with nothing. For higher end cameras offering 4K, 6k and 8K, still frames can often be pulled from the footage, so just get the video right.

With video especially, you will want to use manual exposure and have your histogram on. If it is really sunny, exposure at the surface can be tricky

and shouldn't be left to auto settings. Also, the auto focus from a video camera can tend to wander in and out, even with something as large as a whale. Try to use focus lock or manual focus to prevent this. Water movement combined with whale movement and light rays from above can fool even the finest autofocus system.

GoPros are great for videos of whales underwater, since they are both wide angle with a fixed focus and fixed aperture sports cameras. Unlike a DSLR or mirrorless camera in a u/w housing, GoPros are the underwater version of a point and shoot. On the plus side, stabilization technology and quality was greatly improved with the HERO 7 Black and 9 Black. If the only camera you have is your phone, shoot video and pull out an action frame for a still.

Use the best combination of shutter speed and stabilization your camera can offer. With both video and stills, you may be swimming pretty hard to keep up with even a whale that is just cruising. SloMo helps steady a clip.

A whale breaches near Kona's "Whale Grounds"

First Encounter - Humpbacks

I have lived in Micronesia for decades now and have had the great fortune to have seen a lot of wonderful things in the sea. Submerged, coral-encrusted war wrecks, shark infested points and walls drenched in color and marine life and remote atolls with reefs rarely touched by man. But we don't have many whales out here. Only on rare occasions and far out to sea do we usually see them.

I was bemoaning this fact quite a few years back to my friend Jim Watt and he told me to come to Kona for a week to visit him at his home and he'd show me

whales up close and personal. Sadly, Jim passed away recently but when he was healthy and in his prime, perhaps no human on Earth loved to cavort with humpbacks and other blue water denizens more than Jim. Jim's special gift of being to expertly free dive and photograph whales underwater combined with an uncanny knack of shooting amazing whale breaches had made him pretty much world famous and internationally published.

I quickly snapped up the offer and soon was sitting miles offshore Hawaii on a sea of glass. The island was a speck in the distance. Nothing but gin clear water and an occasional bird was out here.

Jim told me these were what he dubbed "The Whale Grounds" and that he had success photographing whales out here more than any other place. On the first day, we heard the sound of whales blowing as they surfaced and looked to see five males traveling toward us. He told me to lower myself in the water and I looked down to see the whales traveling right under the boat. I was awestruck. I was so enamored by the scene I didn't even snap a photo. I just watched as this group slowly swam by, probably on the way to find a female to court.

Jim told me of his several whale encounters, fueling my enthusiasm as the days went on. He coached me a bit on photographing them and we spoke of cameras and life. It was a fine week.

What sticks in my mind was the first time I saw a baby whale calf nursing from its mother. Jim explained to me that adult whales will rest 30-60 feet below the surface. They can hold their breath for 20-30 minutes but the calf is usually only good for eight minutes or so. They rest underwater and just drift along in the ocean currents

We located a mother and calf. We stopped the boat. I slowly and quietly slipped in to the water and Jim quietly motored away. I was alone in the vast sea and hung there and looked down into the big blue as light rays danced.

A mother nuzzles her calf off Ha'apai

Mother and calf in Tonga

There, below, was a touching sight. Mother was sleeping and under her large pectoral fin was her tiny calf. Receiving milk and looking so protected by her large mother, the calf was safe and satisfied. I was mesmerized. I had never seen such a tranquil and precious image in Nature.

Soon I saw the baby move and the calf started to rise. It came near me and surfaced. It took a breath and came even closer. It frolicked a bit, and took another breath. Alone. Free. Vulnerable. Beautiful. Then it started back down and soon it was nuzzling mother again, suckling her teat and reveling in the protection of her watchful mom. This continued for another ascent/descent from the calf and then the next time, magically, mother and baby rose up.

Coming right to me, they surfaced as one. I could not believe the size yet gentility of the mom. She kept a watchful eye on me but did not flee. For the world's largest mammals, they can be skittish and also protective.

They rested and took some breaths and then down they went. I watched this cycle for more than an hour, drifting with whales and not a care in the world. The sun started to sink and we reluctantly made our way back to land, leaving the whales to drift. Thanks to this touching scene and Jim's great knowledge, I was hooked on whales.

Nowadays, humpback whales in Hawaiian waters are heavily protected and only a few licensed biologists can legally get in the water with humpbacks in that state. But it is legal to join them

Whale photography guru Jim Watt feigns a "selfie"
(Photo courtesy David Fleetham)

in the Kingdom of Tonga and also in some places in Tahiti.

Every time I enter the water in Tonga seeking to photograph and observe these special marine mammals, I think about the generosity of Jim Watt. He unselfishly shared his knowledge of the whales and I got know, firsthand, his zest for recording the images that still thrill people around the world. Those moments spur me to continue shooting the wonderful humpbacks in our seas.

I have travelled to Okinawa, Zamami, Mozambique, The Silver Banks, Great Barrier Reef, Ogasawara, Saipan and a few others. But Tonga's relaxed atmosphere and special whale tribe keep calling me back. I thank Jim for getting me into this great passion.

My first "underwater" whale photo taken by hanging from the aft of Jim's boat off Kona.

Tongatapu

Tongatapu, known as the 'Sacred South', is Tonga's main island and usually the starting point for exploring many of the other islands in the Kingdom. It is, for sure, where whale adventures begin. Nuku'alofa, the capital of Tongatapu, and the hub for international arrivals, is located on the north-central coast, and is an active little town with a touch of traditional Tonga and modern Tonga all mixed into one rather charming and laid back melting pot.

Around 70,000 people live on Tongatapu, and Nuku'alofa – translated to 'Abode of Love' in English – is a promising introduction to the Kingdom.

Now if you are arriving on a morning flight and traveling on to some other island or resort, all you see of Tongatapu may be on the short trip from Fua'amotu International to the nearby domestic terminal. But, if you have had to fly a long way to get to Tonga, as many people do, there are many nice hotels and restaurants here. You can get over the jetlag, have a proper meal and night's sleep (even do a bit of exploring) and prepare to start your adventures.

The trip into town from the airport is a nice drive through a few villages and then along the coast and into town. You will see ferries and trading ships dot Nuku'alofa Harbor as you drive in. These are the lifeblood of Tonga with most preparing to venture to the other population centers of Vava'u, Ha'apai and Niuas island groups to the north.

Now if you are staying here, make sure to rent a car or arrange for some tours and have a look around. You will find some restaurants in town and many

Courtesy Google Earth

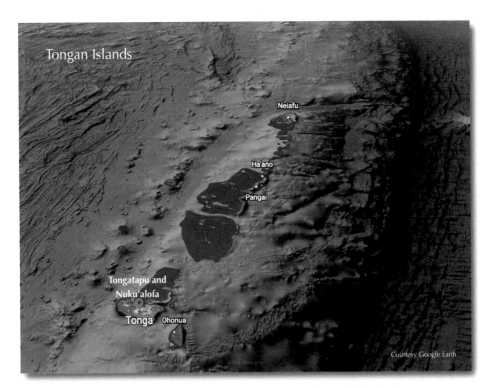

Tongan Islands

Neiafu

Ha'ano

Pangai

Tongatapu and
Nuku'alofa

Tonga Ohonua

have WiFi so you can catch up while you eat. Then near town center is the Talamahu market. This is a fun local affair selling everything from large tapa pieces, fresh fruits, vegetables, hats that say 'Tonga' and some very cool Tongan arts and crafts. While whales are protected in Tonga, there is still some whale bone around from the whaling days and some carvers offer beautiful pendants and other items made from this antique bone. Other intricately

Royal palace and grounds near the coast in Nuku'alofa

Mapua 'a Vaea blowholes stretch down the coastal shore.

carved items like Polynesian fish hook and whale mother and calf pendants can also be found made from cow bone. Wooden items include carved pigs!

On Sundays, the churches of Tongatapu glow with soaring harmonies and a warm welcome to visitors. If you have finished your whale watching and have come down to Tongatapu to catch a Monday flight, Sunday is a good day to rent a car and go for a drive to the famous sites both natural and manmade.

Tongan history includes the ancient Langi (terraced tombs) of the Tongan kings, which can be found in town and at other island locations. More recent are the Tongatapu landing sites of Abel Tasman and Captain James Cook. Plan your day and you can take in a lot.

Stock up the day before as nothing will be open on Sunday until later in the evening. I frequently stay at the Little Italy Hotel (which has hire cars). It does not open it's restaurant until Sunday evening but does provide guests with a variety of Sunday breakfast items in room.

The Mapua 'a Vaea (The Chief's Whistles) blowholes represent Tongatapu's more rugged natural beauty. If the surf is right, this is one of those spots not to be missed. That's because this is not just one blowhole along the coast but a series of maybe a couple hundred that run 3 miles (5km) down the coastline. On windy days with big swells, some of the blowholes have gushers shooting 100 feet (30m) into the

The natural land bridge Hufangalupe is in the southeast part of Tongatapu. It was formed when the roof of a sea cave collapsed.

Mother and calf swim off with the escort nearby

air. It's a feast for the eyes and ears. Salt spray is everywhere so make sure you keep your camera covered in some way to protect the fine salt mist from getting into places where it shouldn't.

Tonga is also famous for its sacred fruitbats. There is one spot they like to roost in the village of Kolovai, up near the western tip of the island. They cling upside-down in the trees in the hundreds. There is no sign to indicate where they are. The trees seem to be on someone's property. So, just drive slowly through town and look up into the tall trees and you should see them.

Since you are now here, you may

Fruitbats are sacred in Tonga as they are considered possessions of the King. They are seen here in the village of Kolovai, near the western tip of the island. Inset: Colorfully dressed lady in Nuka'alofa.

want to get a bite to eat. Some resorts in the area do serve lunch on Sunday and they can be found along the beach road that heads toward the island's most westerly point.

If you are into ancient architecture, what is said to be the South Pacific's Stonehenge, the Ha'amonga 'a Maui (Maui's Burden, see P.8) trilithon is near Niutoua village. The structure consists of three large coralline stones, each weighing about 40 tons, arranged into a trilithic gate. Mortized joints ensure the top stone won't fall off... the same as

Stonehenge!

Whale charters are available here as there are licensed operators. Many visitors combine other adventures with whale swimming in this gateway to Tonga as there really is lots to do. Some resorts are very small and private. Some are on the main island and some on the small islands nearby. They can arrange whale swimming, diving or both as part of your stay. Many advertise having eco-friendly whale encounters. Discuss your needs in advance with the operator to ensure you have fulfilling trips.

Courtesy Google Earth

Eua National Park

'Eua

Ohonua

Pangai

'Eua Island

This may not be the first place in Tonga that comes to mind when one thinks of a destination to see whales, but it is such a nature-oriented venue that it logically becomes part of the outdoor experience. It is rugged and hilly and has secluded beaches and is a bit off the grid.

Travelers can fly here on a flight that takes a whole concise seven-minutes from Tongatapu. 'Eua is off the main island's southeastern tip. This flight is the world's shortest commercial airline flight. If you want to feel like you've traveled a bit, the ferry takes longer. It leaves from Nuku'alofa.

'Eua has roughly 5,000 residents and life is simple here. Accommodations are no-frills and affordable and, for the most part, run by resident 'Euans'. Places to stay comprise more of a mix of lodges, guest houses and cabins although a couple may use the "resort" moniker.

As for the whales, since the whales come from the south, 'Eua is in the main path of their migration, making the island pretty handy for a whale encounter. The best time to experience the whales is in the height of the season, from July to October. Some whales stop here and then move on while others spend the whole season. 'Eua has a small number of whale operators compared to Tongatapu, Ha'apai and especially Vava'u. But small groups and personal experiences go a long way in adding to the fun of the experience.

From 'Eua's east side, especially from the Lokupo Lookout and Laua Lookout in the 'Eua National Park, the

Humpback sounding

'Eau has deep, clear water offshore. Here a mother and calf play at the surface

views of the water over the Tonga Trench are superb. This is the main migrating path for whales and people attempt whale watching from the bluffs. The Tonga Trench lies around 6.7 miles (10,882m) below sea level. The deepest point in the Tonga trench, known as the Horizon Deep, is considered to be the second deepest point on Earth after the Challenger Deep and the deepest trench of the Southern Hemisphere. The Tonga trench was formed due to the subduction of the Pacific plate by the Tonga plate. 'Eua is not very far from Horizon Deep.

And geography is 'Eua's claim to fame. Geographically 'Eua is the Kingdom's oldest island. And despite its small population, it is also the second largest in the Kingdom. It is covered with hills and lush rainforest. It is said to have the Kingdom's best hiking with well-marked trails criss-crossing the pristine 'Eua

National Park.

The island has spectacular cliffs, caves and sinkholes in northern 'Eua or one can venture to the rocky southern coastline to watch sea birds soaring in the thermals swirling around 'Eua's dramatic cliffs. The island also has wild horses that are seen around the Laku Fa'anga Cliffs and Rock Gardens sites. Keep an ear open for the call of the Koki, 'Eua's rare red-breasted shining parrot. Ha'aluma Beach, on the southern coast, is great for a swim.

Deep Blue Tonga is the island's only dive operation, so you can have the reefs pretty much to yourself. The shop gives lessons and "intro" experiences and also caters to the more experienced diver. They will take you to Tonga's biggest (and submerged) cave that has an amazing light show when the sun is just right. Cathedral Cave was discovered in 2001 and is the largest sea

Here and below: Rugged shorelines at 'Eau drop straight into the sea

cave in the South Pacific. Considered one of the best dive sites in Tonga, it is an impressive sight at 330ft (100m) long, 165ft (50m) wide and 100ft (30m) deep. They also dive wrecks and there are stunning, healthy hard coral reefs around the Tongatapu area.

Deep Blue and a handful of other 'Eua operators offer anything from two-hour to all-day whale tours, but the norm is a 4-hour morning with a max of 8 people on the boat. Most have a good supply of masks, fins and snorkels for hire but not all. Ask before you book. But, it is really best to bring your own gear for comfort and to make sure you

Photos this page courtesy Tonga Tourism

Mother and calf at the surface

are able to do the swims without borrowing from the guy who just got out of the water. Tonga's water here is also not that warm so bring a 2 or 3mm wetsuit or at least a wetsuit top. There are none for sale on 'Eau. The sun can also be pretty intense out on the sea, reflecting back from the surface. Eco-friendly sunscreen is a must.

Whale swimmers and photographers can expect all of the same action as one would see in the more popular locations. Heat runs, breaching, mother and calf interaction, spyhopping... keep the camera ready for above water action and be ready to slide in when given the "GO" sign to snorkel to see the whales.

'Eau may gain some popularity in coming years. Right now it is a relaxed, natural spot to see whales

Anatomy of a Heat Run

One surface activity, where the term "gentle giants" has no place, is the **heat run**. With testosterone raging at 50 times that of an enraged bull elephant, competitive males strive to eliminate each other while pursuing a female for mating. It is anything goes and one of the most amazing displays in Nature.

Splashes on the horizon are usually the first tell-tale sign. Obviously not breaches, whales are doing something and in Tonga it is likely the sign that a female has come across a male or males that find her desirable. One male may start a song of courtship. The female's escort may take offense to this. Others hear it and realize a female is around. This can quickly trip some triggers and escalate from wooing to threats to aggression and then rough contact.

Often the female sees this is happening, fears for the safety of her calf and takes off. At the Silver Banks one female took refuge with her calf under our anchored live aboard to escape the attention of horny males.

But when she becomes the target of hopeful suitors, she takes off and males follow. While you are in the boat, your captain will try to follow at a safe distance as the male actions can become quite unpredictable.

Male humpbacks battling with all of their brawn in a heat run

Huge blows signal a threat to another male

Usually the chase will stop and the males will face off. Violent blows from fins and tails take place beneath the surface. Big water blows, surface slaps with tails and fins and a lot of bumping and splashing ensue. You will not be allowed in the water as these males are not playing around. My friend, pro whale photographer the late Jim Watt, once told me he thought it would be a good idea to try to go in the water and shoot the fighting. But after giving it a try, he then told me it is not so smart after all!! Most captains probably won't let you go in as the males are pretty charged up.

The myth about whales always knowing where a human is and not running into a human is not as true as one thinks. I have a photographer friend with nasty barnacle scars to prove it.

These heat runs can last hours and cover miles and miles of ocean. Before you realize what's happening, this incredible combat is already past you, disappearing rapidly into the distance. After a while, the captain's attention will normally turn from pursuing the heat run to finding gentler whales.

Females also don't mate every year. Males on the other hand, spend more time at the tropical areas looking for

Here a group of males confronting one another with contact and blows

chances to mate. The result is usually that there are far more males than females in the mating grounds. In an active year with a lot of whales coming to Tonga, this usually means the chances of seeing one or more of these heat runs are good. They are also called a "rowdy bunch".

Humpback whales do not form long-term relationships. Instead they mate with various different partners. But they do seem to be very picky about who they mate with. This is a dynamic called "mate choice" and it (cont'd P68)

During a heat run fight, one male crashes on top of another

Heat Run by the Numbers

It starts something like this (1) when a male escort hears a song from another male and blows air bubbles signaling his displeasure. If the female has a calf, she fears for the baby's safety and gets it by her side.

Often the female will want no part of this if the calf is young. She will take off with the baby trying to ditch the amorous males (2). The escort will follow, scoping his competition as he tries to keep up. If she loses them, all the better. But they are good at pursuit.

Above you see the whales giving chase. Soon, confrontation will begin.

When the males tangle it is serious business (3). One may crash his head upon another. Flippers covered in sharp barnacles are swung. Tails are lobbed and thrown at opponents. Blood may result from a major hit. The water churns and the battle can last for miles and hours. The female will do her best to escape the fray, protecting the calf from aggressive males, but the males will pursue as they fight.

(cont'd from P66) seems to be a very important factor for reproduction.

By spending lots of time feeding in summer, a female humpback has already taken a step towards reproductive success. For a male humpback to have the most success with reproducing, he needs to mate with as many females as possible. At the same time, however, males spend tons of energy fighting each other to win one of the few females. If they have to fight to pass on their sperm, then they will fight for the fittest mother for the best chance at healthy offspring.

The males can travel great distances for long periods of time or stay in an area circling for hours - but generally they are on the move and this is how the heat run develops, as other whales join in along the way. If you are in the water you may hear a distant song or cry. You may not see another whale but all of a sudden you may see the male escort of a mother and calf begin to blow bubbles and get somewhat rigid. This is the beginning. If you are a photographer, the surface activity can make some pretty amazing video or stills, especially with a drone. This is one of Nature's most spectacular mating rituals and your captain should have his eyes on the horizon to try to spot one for you.

Male separates calf
from the mother

4

I was whale snorkeling with Douglas Hoffman when we were fortunate enough to see the finale of a heat run we had been following. This large male (above) had rebuffed all this female's suitors and is now concentrating on mating. He separates the calf (4) from the mother so she will cooperate with him. You can see his penis (5) appear and become erect as he forces her deeper into the clear water.

5

Preparing for intercourse, the male
steers the female down

We watched as he continued to force the female down (6). I snorkeled down to about 20 feet (6m) and I could see them continue to head down even deeper. As I snorkeled up, I realized the calf was being left behind. It went to the surface and then tried to find mama, no one was there (7)... except Doug and me. So instead of going down, the confused calf swam to Doug and me. Suddenly, we were parents!!

6

The couple disappears as the calf heads up to take a breath

Douglas Hoffman is the
baby's new best friend

7

This encounter took place in Vava'u and we had heard that a week before a lone
calf was also seen swimming without its mother. It was eventually re-united. Now,
we were in the same position... suddenly our new best friend was a large and
lonely whale calf. Although it came close, we tried not to touch it, fearing the
mother may reject it. We decided to wait in the area and also alerted our captain to
look for two whales surfacing so we could swim the calf to the mother.

Baby whale swims
close to us

After a while the couple emerges from the depths

Upon surfacing one could see the male penis still out

Finally, the amorous couple emerged from the depths (8) with the aftermath of the liason in the depths fairly obvious with the large male's penis still extended (8a). The baby was nearby and a joyous reunion (9) took place and the male did not interfere. Then they headed to a reef to rest (10).

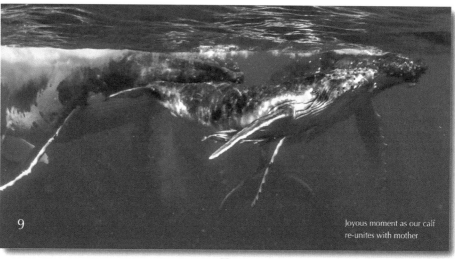

Joyous moment as our calf re-unites with mother

Spent from the exhausting heat run and then mating, the
adults find a shallow reef area to have a well-deserved nap.

Double sounding near a Ha'apai beach

Ha'apai Group

This central area of the Kingdom is truly perfect for beach people and water lovers. The highest isle is Kao, which is almost 3,440ft (1050m) above sea level. The rest of the islands are low and right down by sea level. Most have stunning beaches with graceful palms blowing in the breeze and not a footprint in sight. Only 17 are inhabited. Beautiful hard coral reefs hold all sorts of marine life, from manta rays, sea turtles and schooling fish to soft corals and fun little invertebrates like mantis shrimp. The reefs are quite diverse. And the sunsets can be truly jaw-dropping.

The flight in from Tongatapu is a brief but scenic 45-minute cruise over an open stretch of sea. Then, one islet after another appears below as the plane heads up along this group's eastern side

Amazing Ha'apai sunset

to Ha'apai's capital. Your pilot approaches a tiny airstrip that looks from the air like he's trying to land on a postage stamp. Down you go and within minutes, you are taxiing and about to set foot on Pangai.

There is also a weekly

Banded sea snake

Snorkeling among Ha'apai's coral gardens

ferry but it is not a direct shot. Ferry riders from Tongatapu have to visit Vava'u first and then ride back down to Pangai's ferry landing. It is a 23-hour trip vs. 45 minutes by air.

Ha'apai is the Kingdom's central island group of 62 islands. Isolated, it is just beginning to be discovered by tourists. This tropical paradise is full of possibilities and usually, in season, a nice selection of visiting whales.

When you land on Lifuka Island at Pilolevu Airport, the reaction is kind of "Where is everybody?". Since there are only about 2000 or so people on the island, things are simple here. In all of Ha'apai there are only roughly 6000 people total. So things are pretty basic all over this group.

You take Hala Holopeka Road into

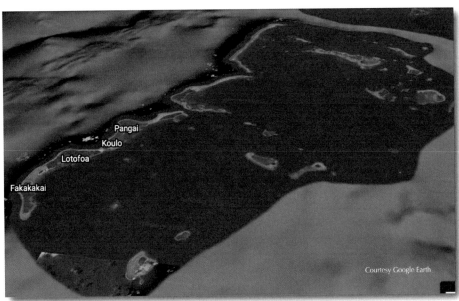

Pangai
Koulo
Lotofoa
Fakakakai

Courtesy Google Earth

The highest point in Ha'apai is Kao Island

Some of Ha'apai's beautiful table corals

Small stingray on the sandy bottom

Lifuka town. It is small and has but a few stores, a bank and ATM and some hostels. The hostels have simple menus, drinks and wifi. And, of course, there are churches. The village center is near the Catholic Church.

It is wise to have some Tongan cash here. Most likely, only resorts will take plastic. Also, bring a proper supply of any special meds you may need. No pharmacy here.

Folk staying on Pangai usually stock up on snacks and such in Lifuka, then go off to one of the nice resorts on the island, on nearby Foa (via the Foa Causeway) or to one of the other isles close by.

Travellers can fill in the day with endless water and some land activities like hiking, sailboarding, snorkelling, kayaking, SUP exploring and diving. There's even horse riding along the white sandy beaches. The place is pretty idyllic.

This lagoon is vast and you may never make across to the west to see or climb

Waiting for word to slide in to photograph humpbacks in Ha'apai

Kao. There are island groups within the Ha'apai Group like Kotu Group, Nomuka Group and Tofua. Whale Discoveries operates a wonderful charter catamaran here and that may be the best way to get around the entire island group. If you come with friends who have their own boat, that is another way. Otherwise, you may have to discuss longer trips and the boat/fuel costs with your resort's whale swimming operator.

If you get a chance, it is worth visiting some of the other inhabited islands just to get an idea of the subsistence lifestyle that Tongans have here. You must ask permission but that is usually no

Girl with her bike and a pig in the outer isles

problem. Ha'apai has roughly 17 islands that have people and small villages on them.

Once at a main village you may notice something a bit odd. The village will have a rather substantial wall or fence around it. All of the jungle along the trail from the beach to the village will be lush and green. But, once inside the compound or enclosure, you will see homes nicely kept with flowers, a school, probably a church, a small government building and kids riding bikes and having fun. AND, you will see pigs pretty much everywhere from giant

Manta rays photographed near Uoleva island's southern tip

Mantas in mating mode at Ha'apai

Sunset lights up chromis and staghorn corals in the lagoon

Piglets follow mom

boars to tiny piglets. Suckling pig and other pork dishes are a big deal in the Tongan diet and also for celebrations. To keep their crops and the natural habitat of the island safe, the islanders choose to keep the pigs fenced in with them. If not, pigs will root around everywhere on the island, destroying taro and other deep rooted crops like yams.

Village people don't see many tourists and those who are comfortable with English will probably strike up a conversation and even offer you a fresh coconut to drink. Take the time to watch them fish or work in the gardens. There may be a small store or two that sells a few canned goods, but otherwise, these folks have learned to live off the land just like their ancestors. They are carrying on a tradition as old as the Kingdom itself.

If you really want to get away from it all, one resort offers a Robinson Crusoe experience where you can stay in a Tongan fale and have an entire island to yourself for ten days. Want to unplug? Want to disappear from the grid? Want to become one with Nature? Ha'apai!

Mother and calf slowly swimming the calm and clear inner channels of Ha'apai

As far as seeing and photographing whales goes, Ha'apai has its share of them and the beautiful reefs can lead to interesting swimming and photographic backgrounds if you come upon cooperative whales.

One encounter I had was swimming in an inner channel with mother, calf and escort. Mother was okay with snorkelers and baby was curious. As we watched the whales, we missed the fact that we were slowly but surely drifting out of the calm channel and into a current feeding another. Soon, we were zipping along at a couple of knots in an amazing drift snorkel. But instead of leaving us, the whales joined in and there we went, zipping down along a wall and reef with humpbacks flying

along just as fast as we were. They even turned around, swam into the current and went for another ride and caught up with us again. Whales know how to party! As we coasted into an eddy, they finally bid us farewell. It was one of the most amazing and fun ocean experiences I have ever had.

In Ha'apai I have also seen some whales do a graceful courtship ritual I can only liken to an undersea ballet. It is beautiful to watch. Prior to that I had only seen this behavior in a rare film taken off Ogasawara by Japanese photographer Akinobu Mochizuki. And we have watched as mother gives baby breaching lessons. Once the calf got the hang of it, it was unstoppable, repeatedly trying its newfound skill.

Above: A calf repeating its newfound breaching skills and (right) another jump from the same calf seen from snorkeler level, both on a wavy day

One gripe some have had about Ha'apai is that visibility can vary as tidal water moves between the islands. Also, the Hunga Tonga-Hunga Ha'apai volcano way far southwest in the group erupted from undersea in 2014. It has been dormant since then, however, with a new island slowly taking shape. But, for the most part, visibility can be very good in Ha'apai, especially along the islands close to the deep Tonga Trench.

Ha'apai is wonderful for water lovers. Having a great humpback encounter while visiting these waters is truly icing on the cake.

Mother and calf with escort drifting with us snorkelers

Sailboats, ferries and whale boats all muster in the morning at the Neiafu piers

Vava'u

Pig munching grass along the road to Neiafu

Whale buffs are lucky. It is the general consensus that the most comfortable time to visit the tiny town of Neiafu at Vava'u is during the dry season between May and October. It is also considered to be the region's high season and coincides pretty much with whale season. Tonga lies in the South Pacific's unpredictable cyclone alley. But cyclones don't come through Tonga too often. The weather and winds are changeable, but typically Spring (Sept to Dec) brings 3-4 days of windy weather followed by 2-3 days of sun and flat seas. Sometimes it rains at night and cools things off, making for

Courtesy Google Earth

Leimatua
Ta'anea
Tu'anikivale
Longomapu
Neiafu
Hunga
Pangai
Kapa

great sleeping. Normally, the whales start to show up here in the northern part of Tonga about the same as elsewhere in the Kingdom, in late June to early July. August and September are the best months for whale observation.

There are no direct flights from overseas. As with Ha'apai, you have to take a domestic flight. You arrive at Fua'amotu International Airport in Tongatapu, then transfer to the domestic airport and catch a local flight to Lupepapau'u International in the north on Vava'u. Travelers with a little more time on their hands can use the ferry.

Sailboats at anchor in
Neiafu's harbor

Courtesy Google Earth

Some flights to Vava'u stop by Ha'apai en route. Others are direct. Either way, look for the stunning sandy beaches and coconut palms of these islands as you

The mornings bring fresh produce pyramids

Marlin bills with Tongan carving

emerald and aquamarine colored clear waters and fingers of sand pointing at rich coral reefs. The lower islands are located in the south and the main island, 'Utu Vava'u, has high limestone cliffs in the north and central regions. In all, there are supposed to be 61 islands here and they vary greatly in size and composition.

After landing, a simple terminal awaits. You retrieve your bag, then drive into town past copra plantations and a few villages. In town, you can sort out your accommodations and marvel at the sailboats anchored in the main harbor.

A good number of the Tonga Tribe whales come up to Vava'u, attracted by the many bays, protective limestone cliffs and warmer water.

fly by. Winging your way over this region on a sunny day is an eye-popping experience. Enjoy the views of vivid

Watermelons are in abundance at the market

Popular lookout of secluded
beaches north of Holonga village

The entrance to
Swallows Cave at
Kapa Island is large
enough to drive a
boat into

Snorkeling down into
the clear blue entrance
of Swallows Cave

Sailboats can be seen coming and going from the harbor

The other way to see Vava'u is to bring your own yacht, which is a popular pastime for vagabond sailors. Their presence helps feed the seasonal tourism that, along with whale enthusiasts, fuels the local economy.

If you come for the whales, you will find the town pretty busy. Keep in mind that when the yachties and whale buffs come in for these five months, that is pretty much when the people of the island make all their income to stay afloat for the other seven months of the year. Neiafu is pretty much a ghost town the rest of the year. A few people come for diving and the other attractions, but it is nothing like June through October. So if things seem a bit more expensive than they should be, well, people are trying to make all they can before the season ends. Still, prices for most goods, foods and services are not that outrageous, especially considering it is an island and many things have to be shipped in. Islands are rarely known to be cheap travel destinations.

The small mom & pop stores and the Utakalongalu Market are open early if you want to get something to take on the boat like fresh fruits or sandwiches or drinks. This busy market is also another fine place to grab weavings, carved bone pendants, tapa products and other souvenirs.

The town has a couple of ATM locations at the banks, many stores and restaurants as well as a few internet cafes. The main street, Fatafehi Road,

Beautiful table corals and a sandy beach at one of Vava'u's uninhabited isles

Kayaking is a popular way to island hop

runs high above the harbor and the view from many of the restaurants and hotels overlooks the bay and all of the sailboats and yachts. It is a pretty but simple place. There are even a few older wooden buildings that give the streets a lot of character. You can also head up to Mount Talau at the end of Tapueluelu Road, which is a fairly easy but steep hike located across the bay, and get an even more scenic view of Neiafu and it's nomadic fleet.

A major fire and a typhoon changed the density of businesses in recent years. Hotels, homestays and restaurants are a bit more spread out now or located a few blocks back into the residential areas. But all in all, it is still a fun place to explore and look for items like whale T-Shirts by local artists.

By night, you will find groups walking the sidewalks and in the streets heading to eateries and bars. There may be a band playing Tongan tunes or even Rock. There is a good vibe and a lot of people talking whales and retelling their adventures of the day. A kava bowl is bound to be nearby. Even though it is a town, the starlit skies and moon can be seen on clear nights. Things usually wrap up fairly early as most folks plan an early start for another big day at sea.

While a standard whale day may last for six hours or so, departing the docks at 8 a.m. and heading back after 2 p.m., you can negotiate with your captain for an earlier start or even a later start.

Heading out to see humpback whales

Some captains stick to routine while others are more flexible and even prefer different start times, depending on the weather and wind.

You may encounter spinner dolphins on the way out to sea as they seem to like to protection of the inner bays. There are many small resorts too and

While people believe humpbacks don't eat while in Tonga, they may not pass up a meal if it is easy to get. Here a humpback joins sea birds, a fisherman and some pilot whales in feeding on a fish school off Vava'u.

Whale calf at the surface in Vava'u

your whale boat will leave right from the resort.

Each day is a new surprise as one day you may go north along the Vava'u limestone cliffs. The next you may find yourself winding past the southern sandy beaches and islets. The next you may head straight west out to open ocean. Searching for whales can resemble a snipe hunt at times and is always an adventure.

Again, the more you go out and position your self for max time in the water, the better your experiences will be and you may hit the jackpot.

Spinner dolphins leap from the sea spinning and playing

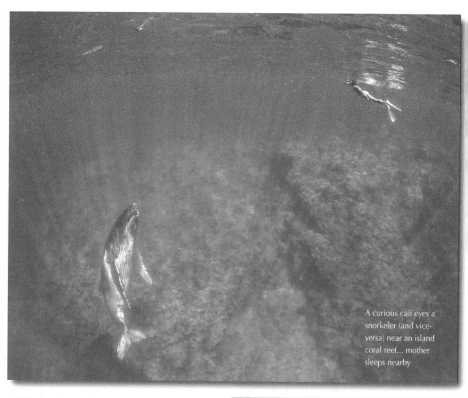

A curious calf eyes a snorkeler (and vice-versa) near an island coral reef... mother sleeps nearby

Of course, the anticipation and then finally getting into the water with the whales is what it is all about. I was amazed at my first encounter in Vava'u. It was windy, spitting a bit of rain and the boat was bouncing around like a cork. One thing I found out early on is that you have to want (sometimes really want) to see whales. No matter what the weather, it takes a lot of search time. They're big but the ocean is bigger. They don't seem to care about what's going on above the water. September weather in Tonga is just the cusp of Spring and it can be chilly. Even though it seems tropical, weather can change quickly here. At times, it's actually warmer in the water than out.

Mother and calf rising for a breath.

From the protection of mom, a baby watches a snorkeler wave hello

Through the coconut grapevine (ship's radio), we were told there was a baby frolicking at the surface and mama was probably down below sleeping. Now when a baby whale "frolics" it makes quite a splash. When we were told to get ready, I donned fins and mask and quietly slipped over the side of the boat.

We found the young whale as the waves rolled over our heads and washed saltwater into our snorkels. But that first close encounter blotted out any discomfort. Cold, waves and salty lungs were all but ignored. Here was something three times my size, covered already in barnacles, wanting to play with me!

Humpback babies can gain up to 150 lbs (70k) a day. So even though this was a "baby" it was like swimming around with a small van with fins. Even though the sky was cloudy and the water a bit stirred up, we looked down and could see the mother resting below. When the mothers rest they stay down about 30-40 feet (9-11m) below the surface for roughly 20-30 minutes at a time before they have to come up and grab a breath. Baby whales have to surface every eight minutes or so. Since a whale calf is usually an only child, I guess they get lonely and want a playmate. So snorkelers may fill this void for the curious calves.

Occasionally the baby would dip down and make sure mom was still there. Then it would come back up, much to our glee, and rocket by. Lifting

Baby hangs close to mom as the escort plays in the distance

a fluke, it came so close I could count the barnacles and see tiny crabs on its mouth. After a while, the considerably larger mother decided baby was having too much fun. She slowly rose from the depths, gathered baby into her breast, cruised by and eyeballed us and, with a few measured kicks of the tails, they disappeared into the blue.

The beauty of the great geography around Vava'u is that you may encounter whales in really shallow water. Sometimes it is so shallow you fear the whale may get trapped. But they seem to know just where they want to be. I suspect they find safe refuge and warm up a bit in the shallows.

By the same token, the deep waters off Tonga are normally crystal clear and perfect for backscatter-free photography. The rays of light dance on the surface then form beams that converge below. These make for pretty images for both still and video photographers.

A female makes a graceful turn, baby staying close

Every day around Vava'u is a great adventure. Sometimes you may find yourself in line with other boats for your turn at a whale swim. But if you are lucky you will find yourself all alone with a willing "family" that wants to play with some humans. Heading back in as the sun sets while travelling through the coconut-lined channels tops off a great day of whale interaction.

Ongo at the helm as photographer Douglas Hoffman shoots a calf breaching

Remembering Ongo

By DOUGLAS HOFFMAN

I had always wanted to swim with whales and having never done it before, I was told Tonga was THE place to do it. Back then in 2006, I was leading dive trips to Fiji and Indonesia. After seeing so many beautiful coral reefs, nudibranchs and frogfish, I was ready to experience being in the water with big animals. And, well, whales are about as big as it gets.

Going to a location and meeting the operators before leading a group has always served me well. So, in 2006, I went there for a few weeks. I chartered a 60-foot sailboat and my friend and fellow marine photographer Mark Strickland joined me for a 10-day cruise of the entire island group. I wanted to experience not only the whale swimming but logistics and facilities in each of Tonga's three main regions.

We flew to Vava'u, Tonga. Before heading out on the boat, I spent a few days talking with all the local operators to get a feel for the range of day charters and accommodations available. Back then, there were only a few companies offering day trips in Vava'u. I had an extra day before the sailing charter and went out with a captain that was highly

Whale swimming
captain
extraordinaire
Ongo at the
helm.

Whales seemed to be attracted to Ongo. We would sometimes swim back to the boat to see the whales playing for Ongo.

recommended. I was able to experience the stunning island scenery, from high limestone cliffs to lush, sandy islets and, in the process, learn how day trips are operated in Vava'u'. That day I went to the local bar and burger joint called the Mermaid.

While eating, I met Aunofo Havea and Jon Boy, and they introduced me to a man named Ongo. He was quite pleasant and very knowledgeable and we sat and talked for hours. By the end of the night, I felt confident about hiring him in 2007. Little did I know that I was hiring a man considered to be the king of whale guides by his island peers. The next day, I got on the sailboat and spent 10 days in the Vava'u area and the Ha'apai island group. The trip ended in Tongatopu. We had a few really good swims in the Vava'u islands and experienced a huge storm in Ha'apai. Overall the trip was quite successful, but, as it turned out, the best part of it was meeting Ongo.

I hired Ongo for several weeks in 2007. Mark Strickland and this book's author, Tim Rock, joined me. The first thing Ongo said was that not every whale is a swimming whale. He went on to explain that by observing their behavior and breathing patterns, he could tell if they were resting, playing, feeding, tracking, singing, or participating in a competition pod (heat run).

Rather than cruise at high speed, Ongo maintained a slow and steady

"I did not question him, and swam back to the boat as fast as possible. I grabbed a towel to put around my hands and picked up my topside camera. Almost at once, the whales breached really close to the boat."

speed, constantly scanning the horizon. His vision was amazing. Ongo normally spotted whales long before we did. Most times he had already been watching them for a while in order to figure out their behavior. When he felt the whales were receptive, he would simply say "Get ready", then move the boat into position and skillfully drop us. Then he would repeat the words that became our Tonga mantra: "Swim, Swim, Swim."

Ongo explained that if we followed or chased the calf, the encounter would end. He stressed that if we stayed together and in the mother whale's field of vision, she would become comfortable with our presence. This was the goal. That was when a mutual interaction would take place so we could float along for hours observing whale behavior.

I chartered with Ongo for several years after that and had many truly incredible encounters. I remember one time, we were floating with a mother and calf for over an hour when I heard him yell to me get back in the boat. He

said the whales' behavior was about to change and they would breach.

I did not question him. I swam back to the boat as fast as possible. I grabbed a towel to put around my hands and picked up my topside camera. Almost at once, the whales breached really close to the boat. Later, I learned that he had observed a male whale coming from far away and he knew the female did not want to deal with an amorous bull. When the female became aware of the male's presence, she breached as if to say go away.

Ongo knew a lot about whales and each day on the boat with him was an education and an adventure. Rough seas, big waves, rain, and poor conditions never dampened his spirit. I remember on one charter there was a research boat in Vava'u getting DNA sample plugs. As soon as Ongo saw the boat, he turned his boat and took us to another area about 15-20 miles away. He knew the whales would be skittish and not tolerant of swimmers.

Another time there was a tsunami

Mother and calf near surface in Vava'u's western waters

northeast of Vava'u. Some damage was done in outer islands. We delayed, waiting on higher ground. It turned out a small but powerful wave did come through Vava'u but was not noticeable in most of our area. One sailboat reported being spun around while coming in the main channel. We did go out finally after getting the all clear and were out about 45 minutes when we spotted a mother and calf. We watched for a while and the whales were not in a hurry and just logging at the surface. We got in the water and slowly approached and to my amazement the mother seemed happy we were there as if she wanted some entertainment for the calf.

We enjoyed 90 minutes and got back in the boat to warm up and give the whales a break. We did not start the engine but just floated. The whales never left us. So we got in the water and had two more incredible swims... I mean really just incredible. It is for days like that we travel to Tonga.

Sadly, Ongo passed away during one of my charters. He had taken a bad fall down the stairs to the dock and had brain swelling and other issues several weeks prior to our arrival. I remember greeting him at the Mermaid pub the afternoon before the charter. But I was shocked when Aunofo, his partner, came to me early that next morning and

Image taken by Douglas Hoffman on one of his swims with Ongo at the helm.

"He would simply say "Get ready". Then move the boat into position and skillfully drop us. Then he would repeat the words that became our Tonga mantra: "Swim, Swim, Swim!"

told me Ongo had passed.

I attended his funeral with a great sense of loss personally and for the whale watching/swimming community in Vava'u.

I will always remember Ongo as being the man who knew so much about whales and was so willing and gracious to share his knowledge. Thankfully, Aunofo and I have become very good friends and to this day I charter her boat when leading my Tonga groups.

Aunofo has all the knowledge and experience just as Ongo did. And, like her partner, she has an incredible spirit. When I am on the boat with Aunofo, I feel Ongo's presence.

- Douglas Hoffman is a Maui-based photo pro who has led many trips for whale photography to Tonga. Website: **https://douglasjhoffman.com**

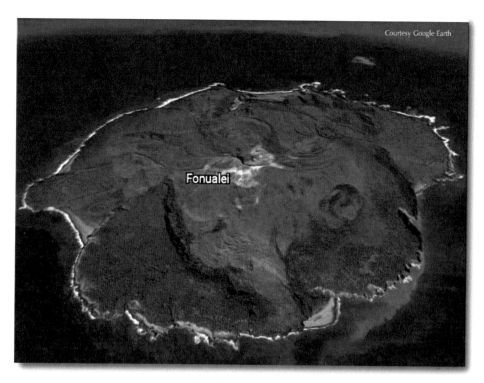

Fonualei

Fonualei, Late, Toku

It is possible to look for whales where few Vava'u boats go but the weather has to really be perfect and you have to have a very reliable boat and even more reliable captain. There are some islands north of Vava'u (Fonualei and Toku) and one more west/southwest (Late) that whales do visit. No people live on these islands. Basically it is mostly birds and fruitbats. And if you go out, chances are that you won't have to line up behind other operators to swim with whales.

So, "Hey, let's go" you say! Not so fast. Once you are away from Vava'u's northern cliffs or western islands, you are out in the open sea with no protection from the weather. Toku is not much more than a sand bar with a bit of greenery struggling to stay attached. Fonualei and Late are larger islands but are far from Vava'u and not the kind of place you want to have to weather a sudden storm with limited gas supply and sketchy radio contact.

So, you need to study the weather well to make sure a smooth trip out and back are do-able. Storms can crop up quickly here. If the captain says it is time to head back, don't argue. Toku, the closest, is roughly 30 miles (54km) out from Vava'u and the highest point on the island is only 26 feet (8m) above

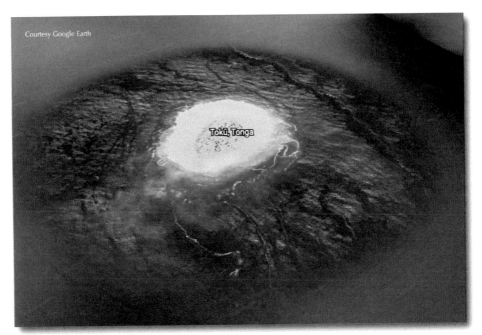

Toku, Tonga

sea level. It has a lot of beautiful white sand, nice beach, low growing green shrubs and some very happy and undisturbed sea birds living there. The south end seems to be a spot where spinner dolphins like to roam. You may

A booby from Toku and spinner dolphins (inset) in the waters around the island

A humpback sounds at Toku's southern end

find them at the bow of your boat if you make it out there and start looking for whales in the area. I have been on trips where we had good luck between Fonualei and Toku, swimming with some single whales... perhaps "teenagers"... and whale trios of mother, calf and escort.

Fonualei is an isolated island about 40 miles (65km) northwest of Vava'u and

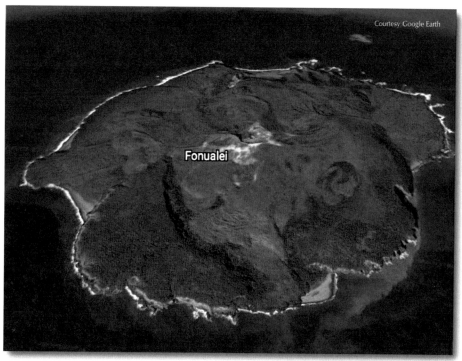

Courtesy Google Earth

Fonualei

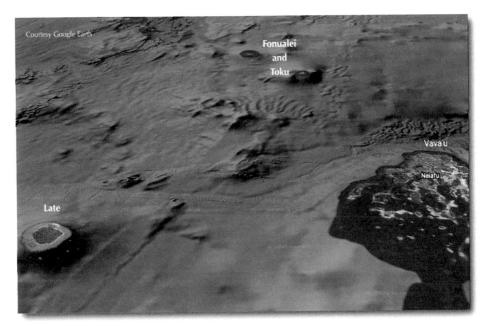

Courtesy Google Earth

Fonualei
and
Toku

Vava'u

Neiafu

Late

ten miles (16km) from Toku. It is a round volcanic cone with a fumarolicaly active crater. Fumaroles are openings in the earth's surface that emit steam and volcanic gases, such as sulfur dioxide and carbon dioxide. They can occur as holes, cracks or fissures near active volcanoes or in areas where magma has risen into the earth's crust without erupting. There are steep cliffs on all but the eastern side of the island and the whole island is basically the volcano. But it has another claim to fame. It supports a recently established population of the rare Polynesian megapode and another globally threatened species, the ground-dove (*Gallicolumba stairi*). Megapodes lay

A whale sounds with Late in the distance

A pilot whale in open ocean near Late

their eggs in soil heated by volcanic ducts. Both Late and Fonualei islands are important refuges for Tongan bird species with Fonualei Island of greater significance for seabirds, which nest there in the thousands.

Late Island is an isolated circular

Two pilot whales and a bottlenose dolphin in the blue water

Whale family cruising by

Mother and calf in the clear, open waters west of Vava'u

island about 34 miles (55 km) west-southwest of Vava'u. The island is also uninhabited and volcanically active but has been dormant since 1854. Late has some of the finest forest to be found in all of Tonga. Late Island has a greater variety of land birds than Fonualei. Coconut crabs, (*Birgus latro*), which are good eating, are also found on Late. The more diverse fauna on Late reflects the greater diversity of habitats found there including mature forest.

Mother and calf rise from the depths to catch a breath

A calf snuggles it's mother at Toku Island

A mobula seen at open sea along the passage to Toku

Pumice rafts are occasionally seen in the waters between the three islands. The eruption spot undersea is most likely an ,as yet, unnamed, unlisted submarine vent or volcano north of Late and south Fonualei. On one occasion we saw what we believe was a pumice raft in the area and also some unusual gathering of humpbacks, dolphins, pilot whales and other marine life like

Humpback mom, calf and escort of Toku

mobulas.

Of course, the whole sea around Tonga is a glorious thing with the deep Tongan Trench not far off and then substantial geographic variations. The

Possibly a pumice raft photographed here in the open sea on a return from Toku Island.

Tongan Archipelago and its marine world can surprise. Getting out to any of these very isolated islands is not a cinch but grab the opportunity if it presents itself. You may see something quite special.

Courtesy Google Earth

The Niuas

Niuatoputao is a flat coral island situated a lot closer to Samoa than Tongatapu. This is not a well-developed place and is not known for whale swimming. For those really wishing to get off the beaten Tonga path, this is it. Located between Vava'u and Samoa, this is called a 'sacred island' and is mostly remote and underdeveloped. The plus is that the water temperature here is much warmer than in the other parts of the Kingdom.

Infrequent Real Tonga flights and some cargo boats and ferries go to the northernmost Tongan islands. With tiny populations and no real tourism accommodations this is really roughing it and it is also really going to a place where getting back is not a certainty. While the name means 'sacred island'

in Tongan, older European names for the island are Traitors Island or Keppel Island. The 2016 census listed 1,232 residents.

Niuafo'ou is the northernmost island in the Kingdom of Tonga. It is a small volcanic rim island with a population of 650. The Niuafo'ou language is spoken on the island

Niuafo'ou, located about 62 miles (100km) west of Niuatoputapu is quite remote even by Tongan standards. From above, it looks like a floating tire. It has a coastline that is rocky and steep, with a few black sand beaches. Niuafo'ou, together with Tafahi & Niuatoputapu island are referred to as the Niuas.

Real Tonga has flights from Vava'u to Niuatoputapu and Niuafo'ou. Flights between Vava'u and Niuatoptapu

A very curious calf takes a long look at the photographer taking this group's photo.

operate two times a month taking approximately and hour and ten minutes. Flights arrive at Mata'aho Airport which is an unsealed coral strip. Flights between Vava'u and Niuafo'ou operate once a month and take an hour and 30 minutes or so, landing at Queen Lavinia which is a grass strip airfield. You should know that flights are likely to be cancelled in bad weather. Also, they are often fully-

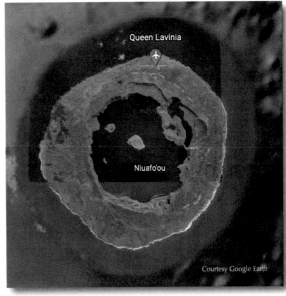
Queen Lavinia

Niuafo'ou

Courtesy Google Earth

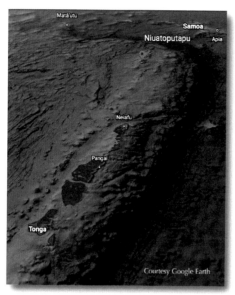

Courtesy Google Earth

booked months in advance and cost approximately TOP$300 one way.

The Friendly Islands Shipping Company runs a ferry service to Niuatoputapu and Niuafo'ou usually once a month, but schedules are erratic and need to be checked with the FISC or with the Tourism Information Centers. Ferries will typically depart from Vava'u on a Tuesday afternoon and take approximately 16 hours to reach Niuatoputapu. The service then continues to Niuafo'ou on a Wednesday evening taking approximately 12 hours, before the ferry makes its way back to Vava'u. Sailings are on the MV Otuangaofa which is a slow cargo ship. Prices are around TOP$215-$250 one way.

So what's Plan B? Most visitors to The Niuas go there on their own sailboats. Some yachties will take a passenger or two along so you can ask around in

Vava'u if you are set on going and have the time to explore. There are anchorages at both Niuatoputapu and Niuafo'ou.

Humpback Whales do come as far as The Niuas during their migration. They actually go even farther north into Samoan waters. Whales can sometimes be spotted from the beaches of Niuatoputapu and the coast of Niuafo'ou, while many yachties also find themselves seeing curious whales that come right up to their boats.

There is no public transportation in The Niuas nor rental cars. Hiking or hitching a ride with the residents is the way to get around. Some vans are the local taxis and carry people around Niuatoputapu and Niuaofu'ou for a small fee. Have cash for this. There are roads and tracks circling both islands.

Vai Lahi means "Big Lake" and it's a large freshwater lake sitting in the crater of Niuafo'ou Island. The lake sits 75ft (23m) above sea level and contains four islands, one of which is sometimes submerged depending on the water levels. Most of the inner walls of the lake are covered in forest.

This is a beautiful but rugged place for wildlife-lovers and birdwatchers. The Tongan megapode is known to use the warm volcanic soils of Niuafo'ou to incubate its eggs, rather than nesting. it was very near extinction but is now rebounding and is most commonly sighted on the central caldera of Niuafo'ou.

Sunbeams rain down on a playful humpback calf and its mom

Tonga, the Friendly Isles

So that just about wraps it up from north to south in this Kingdom of the Whales. Most folks will not get to the super remote isles in Tonga but will pursue their whale fantasies in the three most populated areas. After all, a holiday is about having fun in comfort for most folks and Tonga will be enough of an adventure without having to stray way off the beaten path.

Some will be super serious and devote every waking moment to getting in the water with a humpback. Others will give it a try, hopefully get lucky and then explore other aspects of the Kingdom. As we have pointed out in this book, even though we have written mostly about whale swimming and photography, there are many other aspects of Tonga. Cultural exchanges, food discoveries, viewing craftwork, historical sites, hikes and horseback rides, birdwatching, scuba diving, swimming, escape to a resort island and so many more activities await those who intend to make the trek to the Tongan Islands. I have been able to enjoy many of these and highly recommend trying them on your layover or flying days or even days when your trip is cancelled for bad weather.

That said, swimming with whales can

be a life-altering experience for some. There just is no real way to describe what goes through one's mind when you interact with a massive whale and feel a connection with this smart, well-adapted marine mammal.

We encourage you to seek operators who are serious about being eco-friendly and who take pride in following the guidelines set out for the safety and benefit of both the whales and the swimmers.

So much is being learned about whales now and there is really a lot more still to discover. Whales pass down knowledge from generation to generation, teaching everything from buoyancy and feeding skills to forming complex relationships with other whales and groups to feed and seek food. They communicate with their babies from birth. There is really so much to learn about these mammals. They don't build buildings or have a written language, as humans do. They have no need for such accomplishments with their nomadic lifestyle. And they communicate on a level that may be far more sophisticated than man. The whale brain is larger than a human's brain. It is developed in areas related to sensitivity to sound, impulses from facial areas and social interaction. Some scientists say those large brains house an intellect greater than, but decidedly different from, man.

It is up to us to respect and protect them and the seas they live in. We may just be beginning to learn something pretty special from whales. A trip to Tonga will convince you this is true.

Mom, escort and a fairly young calf (note white color) in the waters off Toku.

The 50 Best Dives Books

We hope you enjoyed this book. Check out our **Top 50 Guides**.
This series is available on Amazon, Apple, Blurb and Kindle.

The 50 Best Dives in Micronesia

The 50 Best Dives in Indonesia

The 50 Best Dives in Japan

The 50 Best Dives in The Philippines

The 50 Best Dives in Hawaii

Mother and calf
humpback with a
plethora of remoras
off Vava'u

Final Thought - Whales are important for the oceans for a number of reasons. What we don't know is the ongoing impact of climate change on whales and their prey, now and in the future. The oceans are already degraded. We do know that humpbacks have and pass on forms of 'culture', including songs and bubble feeding methods. Also, whales are an important nature-based solution to capturing carbon from human emissions. Wherever whales are found, so are phytoplankton. These creatures produce every second breath we take, contributing to 50% of all the oxygen in our atmosphere. Whales are good for the seas and good for man. We need to do everything we can to ensure they thrive. - *Tim Rock*

Made in the USA
Columbia, SC
21 August 2021